Original title:
The Band Around Your Soul

Copyright © 2025 Creative Arts Management OÜ
All rights reserved.

Author: Eleanor Prescott
ISBN HARDBACK: 978-1-80586-022-8
ISBN PAPERBACK: 978-1-80586-494-3

The Chorus of Hidden Dreams

In whispers of giggles, they dance and twirl,
A melody wrapped in a playful swirl.
Lost socks and cats sing a bouncy tune,
Under the watch of a wobbly moon.

With spoons as microphones, they take the stage,
Riding on rhythms that never age.
A chorus of dreams in the backseat ride,
Each laugh echoes where secrets abide.

Unbreakable Ties of Sound

Jumbled tunes in a sock drawer wait,
All humming together in laughter's fate.
The dog joins in with a bark or two,
While the goldfish swims to an offbeat hue.

The curtains sway, like they know the song,
As mismatched socks sing they've never been wrong.
An orchestra built from everyday things,
Creating joy that a silly heart sings.

Lyrical Reflections of the Soul

In daydreams, a comet takes flight with ease,
Spinning tales in the crook of the breeze.
With each little twirl, a confetti pop,
Needle and thread wound in giggles non-stop.

Tickles of music in the garden hide,
Where dandelions play tag with the tide.
The sun throws a party, the clouds join along,
In the realm of reflections, nothing feels wrong.

The Unheard Symphony of Being

A symphony sung by a sandwich and fries,
With pickles on clarinet, to everyone's surprise.
The teapot bubbles a wacky refrain,
While rubber ducks float, dancing in the rain.

From under the bed, a chorus appears,
Composed of the laughter hidden in cheers.
The cat takes a solo, all tuned to delight,
In the unheard symphony that plays every night.

Fleeting Rhythms of Life

In a world where time can tease,
Laughter dances with the breeze.
Ticking clocks play hide and seek,
While socks play tricks and make us squeak.

Grab your shoes, let's hit the floor,
Spin around and ask for more.
With every step, a giggle bursts,
As gravity's a prankster first.

Jellybeans fall from the sky,
Leap and twirl, don't be shy.
In this circus, joy will reign,
With whimsy flowing through each vein.

So let's sip tea from silly cups,
And twirl our spoons till laughter erupts.
Bouncing hearts, don't lose your light,
As we dance into the night!

Twinkling Cadences of the Night

Stars have hats and moonlight sings,
Whiskers tickle while the cat swings.
Crickets chirp a merry tune,
As shadows prance beneath the moon.

Silly owls in funny hats,
Wink at dogs who chase their mats.
With a hop, skip, laugh, and shout,
Who knew fun could be this stout?

The night is young, let's have a feast,
With cupcakes shaped like little beasts.
Balloons float with giddy cheer,
Unruly joy is drawing near.

So let's embrace this midnight spree,
With silly rhymes and glee set free.
Under twinkling lights we twirl,
In this whimsical, fun-filled whirl!

Symphony of Unspoken Bonds

In the quiet of the night, we laugh,
Our secrets wrapped in a silly gaff.
Like socks that dance without a mate,
We twirl in jest, it's never too late.

The clocks tick-tock a merry tune,
As silly thoughts take flight like a balloon.
Each glance a note in this playful song,
Together we thrive, where we all belong.

Vibrations of the Deep Self

My thoughts bounce like a rubber ball,
In my head, they giggle and sprawl.
A wiggle here, a shuffle and sway,
We dance like fools who lost their way.

The world around us sways in cheer,
With whispers that only we can hear.
In every chuckle, a spark ignites,
We shimmy through the silliest nights.

The Chorus of Forgotten Yearnings

Comedic dreams tucked in a drawer,
Waiting to laugh, oh, how they soar!
Forgotten wishes serenade the air,
As we play tag without a care.

Beneath the stars, we spin and sway,
With wishes trapped in a light-hearted play.
Each giggle echoes from the heart,
In this chorus, we'll never part.

Intertwined Harmonies

In a tapestry of laughter spun,
We share our tales, oh, what fun!
Twists and turns, our laughs evolve,
Each blend of joy, a puzzle to solve.

Like noodles dancing in a pot,
We find our rhythm, why not?
A silly team of hearts entwined,
In this silly song, joy we'll find.

Cadence of the Heartstrings

In the jumbled dance of life, we're all a bit out of tune,
Humming like a blender, full of chaos, none too strewn.
With socks that don't match and shoes on the wrong feet,
Our laughter echoes louder, a symphony so sweet.

We prance like silly ducks, quacking in the rain,
Our hearts play the maracas, shaking off the pain.
With every clumsy twirl and mischievous grin,
We're crafting silly songs, where the fun begins.

The Pulse of Intimacy

Two hearts like pendulums, swinging out of sync,
Chasing after fireflies, lost in a wink.
Our secrets shared in giggles, not a frown in sight,
We wear our quirks like crowns, shining oh-so-bright.

When the clock strikes laughter, we dance on the floor,
Twirling to the rhythm, opening each door.
With pizza for dinner and cake for dessert,
Every moment's a treasure, nothing feels like work.

Soundscapes of the Invisible

Whispers weave like starlight, across a midnight sky,
We're hitchhikers on laughter, as time slips by.
With tickles behind ears and a wink here and there,
The air is full of giggles, floating everywhere.

We compose a frolic tune, made of silly faces,
Chasing down the echoes in outrageous places.
Our joy bubble bursts, and who knows where it lands?
In the silly soundscapes, we hold each other's hands.

Bridges of Resonant Feelings

We build our bridges out of cheese, oh what a sight,
Dressed in mismatched patterns, like a clown's delight.
Crossing over puddles, splashing all around,
Our laughter is the music, in friendship, we are bound.

With every silly step, we create our own beat,
Proving that connection can be oh-so sweet.
Through jokes and playful nudges, our hearts strike a pose,
In the garden of our moments, pure joy always grows.

Threads Woven in Silence

In a room where whispers dwell,
Threads of laughter weave their spell.
Invisible hands pull us tight,
Tickling fancies in the night.

A wink here and a nudge there,
Secrets spun without a care.
We craft a quilt of silly dreams,
In muted hues, all stitched with beams.

When the world turns loud and bold,
Our quiet threads, they shimmer gold.
A tapestry that tells our jest,
In patchwork verses, we've been blessed.

So let's add more to our charade,
In every corner, game we've played.
With every chuckle, thread unspools,
In the cloak of laughter, we're just fools.

Pulses of Connected Essence

In the rhythm of our giggly beats,
We dance around in tiny feats.
A heart that skips, a pulse that twirls,
A symphony of boys and girls.

With every shared, ridiculous sigh,
We synchronize, oh my, oh my!
A pulse of joy, a wink exchanged,
Life's little scripts can be so strange.

When chaos reigns, we let it slide,
Bound together, nothing to hide.
Through ups and downs, we bounce along,
In chaos, we still sing our song.

So come on, join this quirky dance,
Let's twirl our hearts in a silly prance.
For in this space, we're never lone,
Connected vibes, we've found our zone.

Melodies of the Inward Journey

Within our minds, a tune does play,
In notes of weirdness every day.
In curious tones, we hum along,
Finding comfort in the wrong.

Each thought a note, so out of tune,
We laugh and croon beneath the moon.
In melodies both wild and free,
We navigate this mystery.

Our journey's path, a circus ride,
With ups and downs, we take in stride.
In the echo of a silly jest,
We find a cozy, joyful rest.

So let the music lift us high,
Like kites released into the sky.
In every giggle, every grin,
The inward journey will begin.

Resonance of the Heartstrings

Strummed chords of laughter fill the air,
A symphony, beyond compare.
Our heartstrings plucked with every wink,
In silly tones, we stop and think.

A playful tug here, a gentle tease,
We find the notes that bring us ease.
In harmony of little quirks,
We strum the joy that always works.

The rhythm of our blended souls,
In resonant waves, our laughter rolls.
Each chuckle like a vibrant string,
That weaves a tune, and makes us sing.

So gather 'round, let's play our part,
In this playful, rhythmic art.
For life's a song, a joyful spree,
Where every note is you and me.

Vibrant Threads of Togetherness

In a world of mismatched socks,
We dance on bubbles and tickle clocks.
With laughter woven into our seams,
We chase our wildest, silliest dreams.

Like noodles tangled in a pot,
We're a riot—a lively knot.
Each giggle is a thread well spun,
Our bonkers charm, it weighs a ton!

With every slip and every trip,
A tale unfolds, we let it rip.
The silly faces that we make,
Are fireworks in our joy's wake.

Together we sing in a flat-off key,
The world's best circus, just you and me.
So grab your hat, let's all parade,
In this cheerful mess, we're unafraid.

Hidden Harmonies of Grace

In every wink, a secret song,
A melody where we belong.
We stumble through our day's ballet,
A funny jive, come what may.

With pancake hats and jelly shoes,
We sway to tunes that never lose.
A sprinkle here, a wiggle there,
Our hidden notes fill up the air.

When life throws pies, we simply dance,
Each silly tumble a new romance.
With tickles in our giggly heart,
We craft our joys, a work of art.

Through whimsical steps, we share the light,
In harmony, we feel so right.
Dance on, my friend, let laughter reign,
For in our quirks, we've much to gain.

The Unheard Ballad

In the corner, there's a tune,
A silent dance beneath the moon.
We sway and twirl, but none can see,
This secret jig, just you and me.

Each skip and hop, an off-key cheer,
Our laughter echoes, nobody near.
We're the stars of our own plays,
Chasing shadows in funky ways.

With marshmallow dreams and silly feet,
We create a rhythm none can beat.
In this strange ballad, we compose,
Every giggle and snort, it grows.

So lift your snack and join the spree,
In this unseen jamboree.
We're legends in our own right,
Dancing our song into the night.

Melodic Embraces

In a whirl of hugs, our bodies sway,
With each embrace, we steal the day.
We laugh and roll, a crazy crew,
With every hug, we start anew.

Like jellybeans in a candy jar,
Our funny quirks make us a star.
With every squeeze, a tune unfolds,
We're made of giggles and pure gold.

So tap your toes and spin with glee,
Embrace the oddity, wild and free.
We harmonize in our own odd way,
A sweet serenade come what may.

Through silly songs and playful jests,
We find our joy; life's simple tests.
In every hug, a world we weave,
With rhythmic love, we truly believe.

Echoing Sentiments

In the attic of my mind, a song plays,
Melodies dancing through the sun's warm rays.
Each note a giggle, a cheeky delight,
Tickling thoughts, keeping worries out of sight.

Cupcakes in clouds, they swirl and plop,
Whispering secrets, then bubble and pop.
A chorus of laughter, in the hustle and buzz,
Echoes of joy, like bees in a fuzz.

Grandpa's old tunes on a repeat loop,
Sway the furniture, instruct the soup.
Dancing with shadows, the spoons join the game,
Every heartbeat resounds with the same old name.

As we waltz through the quirks of our day,
Tickling the fancies, come what may.
For in this symphony, that's funny and bright,
We find our rhythm, our own wild flight.

The Choir of Dreams

Underneath the moon, a choir does sing,
Dodging the raindrops, flapping their wings.
Bananas in tuxedos, looking quite slick,
Chanting out jokes, oh, what a quick trick!

Jellybeans bounce, a marvelous sight,
Dancing through candyland, pure delight.
Each color a laugh, each flavor a grin,
In this quirky hall, where do we begin?

Tickle me pink is the outfit we wear,
Juggling our hopes with calamity's flare.
Chants of absurdity ripple the night,
As we serenade dreams in the moon's frozen light.

So hold on tight as we spin and we twirl,
In this hilarious jamboree of a whirl.
For laughter is magic, and dreams are the theme,
In this offbeat concert, we live in a dream.

The Pulse of Shared Journeys

Riding on clouds where the zebras play,
Finding old maps in the light of day.
Every step's a giggle, each turn's a twist,
Adventures await that none can resist.

The trees whisper secrets in playful tones,
While bunnies in sneakers dance on their phones.
Sharing our stories with grape-flavored zest,
Each moment together, just like a fest.

Trains made of marshmallows puff out sweet air,
With each puff of laughter, we float without care.
The rhythm of friendship, a syncopated beat,
In this carnival of life, we all find our seat.

So here's to the journey, the chuckles we share,
With a skip in our step and laughter to spare.
For every new path is a song yet unsung,
In this whimsical parade, we always belong.

Serenade of Shadows

In the corner of dusk, the shadows unite,
Playing tag with the stars, a marvelous sight.
Whispers of chuckles drift through the air,
As giggles turn serious with not a single care.

A tree with a hat, an owl with a bow,
Join in the frolic, put on a show.
Lollipops serenade while crickets hum tunes,
Ghosts of the past dance beneath the balloons.

With shadows as pals, we skip through the night,
Trading our worries for pure delight.
Each silly step that we take in our spree,
Creates a echo of joy, wild and free.

So here's to the laughter, to shadows that play,
To the fun in our hearts, come what may.
In this dance of the silly, we find our goals,
With a wink and a smile, it brightens our souls.

Rhapsody of Bonded Spirits

In a world of quirky glee,
We dance upon a jamboree.
With friends as wild as the breeze,
Life's a puzzle, not a tease.

They laugh like hyenas, let it be,
As we sip our cups of tea.
One says jokes are like a stew,
The more you stir, the funnier too!

In mismatched socks, we feel so bold,
With stories too funny to be told.
We twirl and laugh, in silly glee,
A crazy bunch, just let us be!

Through laughter's lens, we see it clear,
That life is better with those near.
So here's to us, the joyful crew,
With hearts that jiggle, and skies so blue!

A Lullaby for the Forgotten

Once upon a time, I swear,
To find a sock, you'd have to care.
It disappeared in a whirl of fun,
A sockless dance, oh what a run!

Dear pillow, hold these tales so dear,
Of missing snacks and silly cheer.
A ghostly fridge that hums at night,
With leftovers hiding from the light.

Our dreams, they float with ice cream cones,
A fuzzy feeling in our bones.
Each forgotten snack is just a clue,
To laughter hidden, and joy anew!

So if you find that cookie crumb,
Remember, friends, to have some fun.
For lost delights, though gone, won't fade,
In the lullabies we've gently made!

The Unbroken Resonance

With friends like these, who needs a band?
We strike up laughter, hand in hand.
A kazoo chorus fills the air,
While off-key notes fill every dare.

We start with tunes of pure delight,
A melody that takes to flight.
But when we sing, it's quite a sight,
Off-pitch harmonies take the night!

We can't quite find the right refrain,
But oh, the joy of sweet disdain!
As every note goes bouncing round,
We find that laughter knows no bound.

So let's embrace this merry mess,
Our symphony of silliness.
In every stumble, every laugh,
We trace our map, our joyful path!

Under the Canopy of Compassion

Beneath a tree of giggles vast,
Where every shadow brings a blast.
We share our woes, then make a plan,
To paint our days in a funny span.

The universe plays silly tricks,
With woeful tales that get us kicks.
A drop of rain, a splash of fun,
We dodge the puddles, on the run!

With hearts so big, we laugh at fate,
In every moment, we create.
A silly dance, a playful shout,
In this canopy, there's no doubt.

So here we gather, just for kicks,
With tales of joy and laughter's picks.
Under the branches, we hold tight,
The bond of humor, pure delight!

Harmonious Reflections

In a world of jumbled tunes,
We'll dance like silly loons.
With pants that squeak and shoes that squeal,
We'll make a joyful, wacky reel.

A toaster sings its morning song,
While breakfast struts and plays along.
The jam will slide, the syrup drip,
As waffles join our crazy trip.

The cats will join with crazy meows,
As we compose our greatest vows.
With laughter echoing all around,
We'll find the music in the sound.

So bring your quirks, your jolly ways,
And let's hold hands in this mad craze.
For in this ruckus, hearts align,
With every note, our spirits shine.

Chiming Between Hearts

A trombone hums a silly tune,
While penguins dance beneath the moon.
With each quirky little hop,
We'll jam until the midnight stop.

A cello struts with rattling bow,
As we all make a grandiose show.
With mismatched socks and hats askew,
We'll laugh and twirl, just me and you.

Our hearts beat with a bouncy cheer,
Like rubber ducks who all appear.
In synchronized and silly sway,
We'll find the joy in every play.

The world can be a comedy,
Filled with laughs and harmony.
So grab your friends, don't be shy,
Let's make this moment really fly!

Musical Reflections of the Soul

In the mirror, a banjo grins,
With silly jokes and playful spins.
As we twirl in mismatched shoes,
We'll laugh, we'll play, we cannot lose.

The spoons would clash, the forks would sing,
Creating joy in everything.
With rhymes that twist and giggles loud,
Our quirky selves will make us proud.

Each hiccup counts, each snort, each roar,
As we create our silly lore.
With every laugh, a cheer will swell,
In this wacky, fun-filled spell.

So raise a toast with fizzy drink,
To moments bright, the ones we think.
With quirky riffs, we'll write our style,
And keep on dancing all the while.

The Intricate Dance Within

A polka dot from toe to crown,
As every step brings smiles around.
With goofy moves and silly grins,
Together, let the fun begin!

The band plays on, a comedy show,
While chickens join us with a crow.
In this wild, mystical affair,
Every heart shines without a care.

With bubbles floating in the air,
And clowns who jiggle everywhere.
We'll spin and twirl, a vibrant spree,
In this grand dance, just you and me!

So let the rhythm guide our feet,
To every beat, our laughter's sweet.
As long as we have mirth, we'll find,
The joy that lingers in our mind.

The Fusion of Soulful Rhythms

When the beat drops and we all dance,
Laughter erupts, a merry romance.
Cheeky moves and silly spins,
Tunes unite us, where joy begins.

Friends gather close, we sway in glee,
A conga line wrapped around a tree.
Offbeat shuffles, missteps galore,
But every mistake feels like a score.

Echoes of chuckles fill the air,
Rhythmic chaos is our shared flair.
In sync or out, we don't really care,
Each quirk adds spice, a delightful scare.

So let's groove, let's shimmy too,
In mismatched socks and colors askew.
When the music plays, our hearts take flight,
Dancing together feels so right!

Cadence of Shared Silence

In a quiet room, we share a glance,
No words needed, we start to prance.
With silly faces and giggles loud,
Our silence speaks, we laugh proud.

Poking the dog and tripping a chair,
Every mishap leads to a dare.
Whispers turn into bursts of cheer,
In this stillness, we're all so near.

Lying on the floor with popcorn spilled,
A silent movie is joyfully billed.
Every glance, a story told,
In this hush, our hearts unfold.

So here's to the quiet moments we keep,
Where laughter's the language, not meant to sleep.
Together we weave a tapestry bright,
In our shared silence, we find delight!

Belonging in a Melodic Tapestry

Gather round, let's stitch together,
Threads of laughter in any weather.
With every note, we form a quilt,
Crafted from joy, no wiggle guilt.

A poky finger, a funny dance,
Unexpected bursts, a wild chance.
Every chord is a cheerful bliss,
Through tangled tunes, we reminisce.

Singing off-key, yet harmony grows,
In a laughter-soaked blend, everybody knows.
Our melody's messy, but hearts stay whole,
Each stitch of joy, that's how we roll.

So grab a friend, let's weave some fun,
In our melodic chaos, we're never done.
Step by step, we dance and sway,
Creating our own sweet, silly way!

Siren Songs of Kindred Spirits

With a wink and nod, we start the show,
Singing off-key, but spirits glow.
Siren songs that make no sense,
Crazy laughter, a joyful defense.

In our little crew, we shine so bright,
Bantering back, through day and night.
Tales of mishaps in perfect tune,
Under the stars, we croon and swoon.

Harmonize with boisterous glee,
Every blunder brings more esprit.
Loud as lions, yet sweet as pie,
Together we shine, you and I.

So come and join this misfit band,
With every laugh, let's take a stand.
Our siren calls echo through the air,
In this silly song, there's magic to share!

Consonance of Inner Worlds

In the attic of my mind,
Jokes and giggles unwind.
Thoughts like balloons take flight,
Bouncing around with delight.

A parade of quirky dreams,
Silly laughs burst at the seams.
Whispers dance with playful glee,
As echoes sing in harmony.

Voices clash like pots and pans,
Turning thoughts in zany plans.
A chorus of the absurd and bright,
Spinning tales by candlelight.

In this circus of the brain,
Every moment's quite insane.
With a wink and a knowing smile,
Come join the fun for a while.

Voices Wrapped in Connection

In my head, a chatty crew,
Making plans for things to do.
Ridiculous schemes like running fast,
Competing for who'll come in last.

Bananas wearing silly hats,
Singing songs to dancing rats.
Every thought a vibrant thread,
Stitching laughter where I tread.

A conference of the absurd,
Where every whim is just a word.
Chattering like a messy parrot,
Nonsense blooms, can't help but share it.

Voices wrap, like warm embrace,
Clashing thoughts in a playful race.
Together they make merry noise,
In this realm of jester's joys.

The Resonant Heartbeat

A rhythm beats within my chest,
Pulsing life with foolish zest.
Each thump a laugh, a silly dance,
In this world of goofy chance.

Heartfelt jokes take center stage,
Modeling love in every age.
A melody of bright surprise,
Twinkling like the stars in skies.

The echo of a cheerful tune,
Makes me laugh from night till noon.
As giggles ring, my worries flee,
In this dance of jubilee.

Together we resonate and play,
Silly stories lead the way.
With every laugh, a heartbeat sings,
Exploding joy in vibrant rings.

A Festival of Inner Voices

A carnival inside my head,
Where all the silly thoughts are fed.
Each voice a float in grand parade,
With laughter and confetti laid.

Clowns that juggle whimsy bright,
Making fun from day to night.
Every quirk a vibrant spark,
In this fest of wild and stark.

Join the dance, the merry throng,
Where every thought is a happy song.
A festival of laughs bestowed,
On ridiculous thoughts that flowed.

Voices mingle, twist, and swirl,
Creating chaos, watch it whirl.
In this carnival we glide,
With smiling hearts, let joy abide.

Dancing Notes of Affection

In a twist of fate, my socks do slide,
While I attempt to dance, I'm filled with pride.
With every shuffle, my toes do gleam,
A pirouette? I think it's just a dream.

The cat joins in, with graceful flair,
As I tango with him, without a care.
A playful leap, I trip and spin,
The neighbors laugh, they think it's a win.

Bouncing notes from my radio blast,
Each silly step, a moment to last.
Laughter echoes through the vibrant air,
Who knew my moves could be quite so rare?

So come and join this humorous spree,
We'll dance together; you, the cat, and me.
With rhythmic joy, let's cause a scene,
In this dance of life, we're all just keen!

Flux of Internal Music

Inside my head, a tune does prance,
It makes me giggle; I can't help but glance.
A rhythm of chaos, a joyful jam,
I trip on beats, I'm a wobbly ham.

Thoughts are like bubbles, they pop and float,
Sailing on wishes, on a silly boat.
Each spluttered note, a comic sound,
In my mind's concert, mayhem is found.

Sometimes it's classic, sometimes a beat,
A polka of nonsense that tickles my feet.
An orchestra plays in mismatched time,
Oh, how I adore this chaotic rhyme.

Welcome, dear friend, to my wild parade,
Life's a jest, and we're all unafraid.
In this flux, let's dance till we cry,
With beams of laughter, we'll soar and fly!

Caress of Celestial Notes

Under the stars, a silly serenade,
Cosmic giggles in a galaxy made.
Planets tap dance in the void so wide,
With starlight whispers, joy must abide.

Comets streaking with winking eyes,
Drawing smiles from the moonlit skies.
A trombone played by an astronaut's hand,
Melodies flowing through this cosmic land.

Galaxies spin in a wobbly beat,
While space-time laughs, it feels so sweet.
Shooting stars, with their luminous trails,
Bring jests of humor in glowing sails.

So here we twirl, my twinkling kin,
In the universe's dance, let the fun begin.
With a wink and a chuckle, we'll explore the night,
In the caress of this laughter, everything feels right!

The Fusion of Soulful Echoes

Echoes collide in a silly embrace,
Wobbling tunes create a humorous space.
Each silly note bursts into song,
In this fusion of laughter, we all belong.

Sprightly whispers bounce off the wall,
As sock puppets giggle, they tumble and fall.
An accordion sputters, sending us wild,
With joyful shouts, like a gleeful child.

Together we blend in a goofy display,
Creating a melody that sweeps us away.
Harmonies clash in a marvelous brawl,
In this nonsensical world, we're having a ball.

Join me in this laugh-filled escape,
As melodies twist in a comical shape.
With a wink, we'll dance through each note's embrace,
In this fusion of echoes, we find our place!

The Symphony of Together

In a world where laughter sings,
All our quirks wear jazzy rings.
We dance to tunes that tickle the mind,
A note of chaos, sweetly unconfined.

Balloons and kites fly high in the air,
With hiccups and giggles, without a care.
Let's sway to rhythms of mishap,
In this comical chaos, we'll happily clap.

Our voices clash like pots and pans,
Creating symphonies only we can!
Through silly moments, we create a score,
In this grand orchestra, we always want more.

So grab your spoons, let the fun ignite,
In a medley of chuckles, everything's bright.
Together's the symphony, striking a chord,
With laughter and love, we can't be ignored.

Refrains of the Heart

With every beat, a giggle starts,
Drumming fun deep in our hearts.
Puppies in hats, a sight to see,
Twisting the melody, just you and me.

We sing with socks that don't match,
A chorus of memories we quietly hatch.
Whispers of tickles, a clever snort,
Each refrain a joyous retort.

Our secrets dance on silver strings,
Witty verses where laughter springs.
In the jam of life, we're silly and bold,
Crafting stories that never get old.

Through the verses, we trip and sway,
Finding the humor in every day.
So here's to our rhythm, a heart's delight,
In the song of together, everything's bright.

Frequencies of the Unseen

In whispers of giggles, we vibrate high,
With voices like bubbles floating by.
A pitch so absurd, we can't help but laugh,
Our jokes go unheard, the world's best gaffe.

Invisible waves bring quirky cheer,
Each chuckle a frequency that draws us near.
We dance like jitterbugs in silly shoes,
Finding the rhythm in our own views.

With every call, our mischief flies,
Like squirrels in tuxedos beneath bright skies.
Tweaking the norm, we discover delight,
Creating our tunes in the soft moonlight.

So tune in to laughter that plays every day,
In this wacky melody, we find our way.
Together we giggle, let the unseen play,
Frequencies laughter can never betray.

Soulful Convergences

In a mash-up where oddities meet,
We twirl like donuts, so sugary sweet.
A chuckle collides with a giggle divine,
Laughter's our glue, and it's oh-so-fine.

With quirks uniting like mismatched gears,
Creating a rhythm that banishes fears.
We tango with tickles and salsa with cheese,
In this dance of confusion, we move with ease.

Our spirits entwined, a plush embrace,
Carrying wit to this quirky space.
Together we tangle, with jokes that unfold,
In this vibrant narrative, our warmth is bold.

So let's celebrate the fun that we find,
In the kaleidoscope of hearts intertwined.
For in the giggles and joy that we share,
Every moment's a treasure, truly rare.

The Quiet Communion of Souls

In a room so small, we laugh, we jest,
The jokes we share, they pass the test.
Whispers float like tunes on air,
Tickles and giggles, banter to spare.

Our spirits dance in silly stride,
With silly hats and laughter wide.
Who needs a stage for grand display?
Our quirky joy's the main bouquet!

In secret corners, we plot and scheme,
Like misfit kids in a wacky dream.
With rubber chickens and silly shoes,
We craft our fun, no time to lose!

So lift your glass, let laughter roll,
In this odd corner, we find our soul!
A quiet league of playful hearts,
In every joke, our humor starts.

Orbit of Echoing Dreams

In the cosmic swirl of bizarre schemes,
We navigate through echoing dreams.
With yo-yos flying, and socks that glow,
Our playful spirits surely steal the show!

Round and round the plucky stars,
We chuckle at our silly scars.
A comet made of marshmallow fluff,
Orbiting laughter, never enough!

Dancing ducks in a cosmic ballet,
Chasing giggles that lead the way.
In this universe of whims and quirks,
Our hearts do cartwheels, and laughter lurks!

So grab a friend, let's swirl and spin,
In this fun ride, let the laughter begin!
Echoing dreams in a joyful embrace,
In our silly world, we've found our place.

Harmony in the Heart

In the land of giggles, we unite,
With silly songs at morning light.
We harmonize with clumsy grace,
A choir of chuckles, we do embrace.

With spoons for drums and voices loud,
We serenade the ever-curious crowd.
Jokes on the breeze, oh what a smart tale,
In the realm of humor, we never fail!

Mixing colors of joy and fun,
In our quirky world, we've already won.
A symphony of laughter, bold and bright,
With every note, we chase delight!

So gather round, let the mirth depart,
In this perfect harmony of the heart.
With laughter as our guiding star,
We weave our joy no matter where we are.

Strings of Affection

Tangled strings of playful cheer,
Bouncing around like we've no fear.
Through ups and downs, we pull and tug,
Every thread wrapped in a silly hug.

From rock to roll, our tunes entwine,
Together we twist like a funky vine.
With every strum, a chuckle flies,
Our goofy bonds spark laughter highs!

Banana boats on a wild wave,
We ride through jokes, that's how we behave.
Strings of mirth connect us tight,
In this playful jam, we ignite the night!

So let your heart-string sing along,
In our funny world, we all belong.
Each note we play fuels the next spin,
Together we dance, let the fun begin!

Resonance of Hidden Dreams

In a world where shadows dance,
Silly thoughts take every chance.
With dreams that giggle, jump, and play,
They whisper secrets night and day.

Clocks tick-tock while socks go missing,
Chasing laughter, never dismissing.
A croaky frog in a polka dot tie,
Sketching rainbows in the sky.

Each pause is filled with goofy cheer,
As clouds pretend to disappear.
With every grin, the world gets bright,
Funny mischief paints the night.

So let your dreams take silly flight,
With wobbly dances that feel so right.
In this laughter-filled parade we find,
A hidden spark with tales unconfined.

Notes from the Core

Inside my heart, a ticklish tune,
Played by a jester in a balloon.
Each note bounces, flops, and rolls,
Revealing the winks of playful souls.

Oh, the melodies that twist and twirl,
Like spaghetti in a wobbly swirl.
They giggle at the serious things,
And fling confetti with rubbery wings.

Accordion sounds and trumpet toots,
Dance like wild, enchanted hoots.
Life's a carnival, silly and bright,
With echoes of laughter wrapped up tight.

So, join this chorus, loud and free,
Of quirky tales by the whimsical sea.
Let your heart hum this comic score,
And celebrate joy forevermore.

Whispers in the Wind

The breeze carries tales so funny,
Like a squirrel in shades, all sunny.
It tickles leaves, a gentle tease,
Bringing giggles from the trees.

A gust will shout a riddle to your face,
While clouds prance, oh so out of place.
"Why did the chicken cross?" they jest,
"Because it saw a squirrel in a vest!"

They race through skies, with fluffy glee,
Telling stories that tickle the knee.
In every whisper, a chuckle lies,
As nature winks with twinkling eyes.

So lean in close to catch the fun,
When breeze and laughter both have spun.
Join in the secrets of nature's relay,
Where joy and whimsy dance and sway.

Tapestry of Togetherness

We weave our quirks into a thread,
Like mismatched socks pulled from the bed.
With every laugh, a stitch we make,
For silly bonds, let's never break.

In gatherings of joy, we twine,
With stories crafted over time.
An orchestra of snorts and squeals,
Where friendship wraps, and laughter heals.

Like jigsaw pieces, not quite right,
We find the fit, and it feels so bright.
So let's embrace the joy we bring,
In the melody of togetherness, we sing.

Through every twist, each silly phrase,
We celebrate in our own ways.
A masterpiece crafted by three or four,
In this tapestry of giggles, we soar.

Harmony of Inner Echoes

In the chambers of my mind, they play,
A raucous tune that leads me astray.
Laughter dances, skipping like a rock,
Echoes compose a grand tomfoolery clock.

Jokes and jigs in melodic embrace,
Prancing about in this joyous space.
Each thought a note, a chuckle to rise,
Conducting chaos beneath vast skies.

Oh, the symphony of silly dread,
A orchestra where none are misled.
Tickling my senses, they romp and play,
In this wild sonata where quirks hold sway.

So let the rhythm of giggles unfold,
In this carnival where fun is our gold.
With every laugh that fancifully soars,
We'll make merry, who needs encore?

Threads of Celestial Melody

Woven with giggles, a tapestry bright,
Stars twinkle wildly, in comedic flight.
The cosmos chuckles, tickled by chance,
As we wobble through this cosmic dance.

Galaxies swirl in a playful embrace,
While asteroids wink in a laughing race.
Cosmic strings pull us with glee and delight,
Bouncing like balloons painted in starlight.

Gravity giggles, pulling us near,
In this celestial theatre of cheer.
With meteors zipping in bizarre formation,
Each spark a laugh, a spectacular sensation.

So let's sway with the glimmering spark,
In this thread of merriment, we'll embark.
Freedom in orbit, let joy take its toll,
As we frolic and spin, heart and soul!

Whispers of the Heart's Ensemble

In the nooks where secrets leap and bound,
A comedic chorus can always be found.
Heartstrings tug with a playful flair,
Whispers of laughter soar through the air.

Like a cat on a piano, they prance,
Tuning into life's whimsical dance.
Each tickle of joy, an unexpected turn,
With every giggle, our spirits burn.

Conversations with shadows, they nod and tease,
Mischief erupts with the greatest of ease.
Painting the mundane with strokes of delight,
We'll draw a smile with all our might.

In this pocket where chuckles combine,
Every heartbeat is a muddled line.
Embrace the joy, let the heart take a stroll,
In this ensemble, there's room for the whole!

Chords of the Unseen

Strumming through life with invisible strings,
Laughter resounds, oh the joy that it brings!
We dance through the moments, so light on our feet,
In this quirky sonata, we find our beat.

A polka of joy, with a wink of the eye,
Colossal giggles soar into the sky.
Tickling fancies with each twinkling note,
In sync with the chaos, we wiggle and gloat.

Invisible hands conducting this spree,
Let's shake up the world with wild jubilee.
Every blunder a chord, incredibly sweet,
As we march on with laughter, can't feel the heat!

So gather together, let silliness reign,
In this concert of life, joy is the main.
With unseen strings, our spirits unite,
Creating a symphony; oh what a sight!

Echoes Within the Silence

In the quiet, laughter rings,
Like a bird that lost its wings.
Whispers dance in silly grace,
Tickling thoughts all over the place.

Echoes bounce like rubber balls,
In empty rooms with silly walls.
A giggle floats on dust-filled air,
As if the silence has a flair.

Silly secrets softly sing,
In the hush where chuckles cling.
Muffled joy that wears a hat,
Turning whispers into chat.

When the silence plays its tune,
It tickles toes like a balloon.
Joy contained within the hush,
Fills the void with playful rush.

Melodies of the Inner Light

A tune that wobbles through the night,
With silly sparkles, oh what a sight!
It dances in a clumsy twist,
Like clumsy feet you can't resist.

Bubbling glee from deep inside,
A melody that cannot hide.
Jolly notes in funny pairs,
Swaying like they haven't a care.

Each giggle shines like a bright star,
A chorus that won't stray too far.
Humming soft, then bursting wide,
With joy that sparkles like a tide.

When the heart learns to take flight,
Through rhythms bright, it feels just right.
Tickling minds with silly cheer,
As melodies draw us ever near.

Chords of Connection

Strings of laughter form a twine,
Connecting folks with no design.
A pluck that sends a giggly wave,
Frolicking hearts, no need to save.

Melodic ties like silly jokes,
Bring together even grumpy folks.
Each chord a bridge, a jolly strand,
Binding us with a touch so grand.

Harmony in every grin,
Where friendships start and never thin.
With playful strums and cheerful knocks,
We dance around like fluffy socks.

The music flows, a bubbly stream,
Connecting us through every dream.
In joyful notes and silly ways,
We share our hearts through funny plays.

Unseen Ties of Love

Invisible threads that make us giggle,
Twisting and turning, never a wiggle.
Love's a dance with a clumsy beat,
A funny shuffle on silly feet.

Laughter binds like sticky glue,
In every hug, there's joy anew.
Giggling hearts, a secret code,
In whispered jokes, our love's abode.

Ties so tight, yet light like air,
A joyful bond that takes us where.
Silly moments shared in fun,
In this wild dance, we're never done.

Through laughs and jests, we ride the wave,
With unseen ties that love will save.
In every chuckle, every cheer,
An endless bond that draws us near.

Cloak of Harmonious Whispers

In shadows soft, we prance about,
With giggles high, we shout it out.
A cloak of laughs, we wear with pride,
As melodies twirl, our joys collide.

Each jingle rings, a playful tease,
We dance like leaves caught in the breeze.
With whispers sweet, we spin and sway,
In this fine cloak, we'll laugh all day.

The beats of joy, they tickle our toes,
In this grand joke, everyone knows.
As harmonies twine like vines in bloom,
We share a laugh in this vibrant room.

With playful nudges, we bump and cheer,
This cloak of whispers draws us near.
So let's embrace this merry thrill,
In joyful cacophony, we fit the bill.

The Locket of Affection

A tiny trinket, so shiny and bright,
Holds secret giggles, pure delight.
A locket swings along with flair,
Unlocking memories floating in air.

Within this charm, a joke is stored,
A twist on love, oh how it soared!
With every flip, a chuckle ensues,
A treasure chest of playful news.

With heartfelt grins, we wear it close,
Spinning tales that matter most.
Each smile a key, in laughter we find,
The warm embrace that's truly kind.

So let's wear stories, not just the gold,
In the locket of warmth, let love unfold.
In playful whispers, our joys unite,
A chain of laughter, oh what a sight!

Embracing the Aether

Through bubbles bright, we float and glide,
On waves of giggles, we take our ride.
With silly hats and wacky grace,
We dance in air, a joyous space.

The aether hums with laughter's song,
Catching each jest, where we belong.
A tickle here, a wiggle there,
In glee we're wrapped, beyond compare.

With colors wild, we swirl and spin,
In this grand game, we always win.
As laughter lifts us high above,
We twirl freely, filled with love.

So take my hand, let's leap and soar,
Into the giggles, forevermore.
In every step, let laughter reign,
As we embrace this sweet campaign.

The Heart's Hidden Stage

Behind closed doors, our antics play,
In this secret space, we find our way.
A stage of whispers, each act a cheer,
Where laughter dances, crystal clear.

With silly hats and clashing shoes,
We strut and fret, we sing our blues.
A comedy sketch, each role a treat,
In the heart's theater, we feel complete.

A cast of dreams, we all entwine,
Creating smiles as hearts align.
With every jab and playful jest,
We turn each moment into a fest.

So come, my friend, join in the play,
Together we'll chase the blues away.
On this hidden stage, we find our glow,
In laughter's arms, we steal the show.

Serenade of the Spirit

In the corner, a ghost does jig,
Wobbling around like a big, old pig.
With a top hat and a dance so grand,
It struts about, a sight so unplanned.

Laughter flows like a bubbling stream,
As spirit friends gather, they all beam.
They twirl and spin, with glee and cheer,
A spectral party, oh dear, oh dear!

They tickle the air with ghastly glee,
Making shadows laugh and giggle with spree.
In every nook, a joke unfolds,
As even the silence has stories bold.

So raise a toast to the ghostly crew,
With a wink and a grin, they laugh anew.
Though they lack a body, they dance with zest,
In this merry party, they're truly blessed.

Melodic Threads of Existence

Strings of fate, a comical play,
Wobbling shadows bounce in ballet.
With a pluck and a strum, they spin around,
In each silly note, joy can be found.

A jester's hat upon the breeze,
Echoing laughter that dances with ease.
The melody sways in a quirky tune,
Underneath a waggish, glowing moon.

Life's tapestry weaves in threads of cheer,
Each stitch a chuckle, drawing us near.
In quirks and twists, the laughter flows,
As time spins tales in goofy prose.

Celebrate the whimsy of every day,
With clinks and clanks, we find our way.
In each playful tune, our hearts combine,
As the strings of existence brightly shine.

The Rhythm of Kindred Souls

Bouncing beats in a funny dance,
Where each best friend finds a chance.
Chasing each other in a silly chase,
With goofy grins lighting up the space.

Hiccups and snorts fill the air,
As spirits jiggle without a care.
Together they twirl in a merry chase,
Every misstep brings a smile to the face.

They wave their arms with a splendid flair,
Making music with echoes everywhere.
In this carnival of giggles and laughs,
Together they write the silliest drafts.

So join the line of happy souls,
With jigs and jives, we reach our goals.
In this rhythm, our hearts unite,
As we dance together through day and night.

An Ensemble of Emotions

A symphony plays with a twist of jest,
Notes of joy that never rest.
Each chord a chuckle, each pause a grin,
In this playful tune, life can begin.

Emotions bounce like rubber balls,
Rising and falling, echoing calls.
From giggles to guffaws, we dance as one,
In this funny ensemble, we have such fun.

Silly secrets drift in the air,
As laughter wraps us with tender care.
In each note played, a story is spun,
In this orchestra, we're far from done.

So let's gather 'round for a joyous blend,
With each heartfelt strum, our spirits mend.
Together we thrive in this playful role,
United forever—an ensemble whole!

The Enchanted Embrace

In a realm of giggles and grins,
A jester spins while mayhem begins.
With socks on his hands and shoes on his head,
He dances through laughter, where whimsically led.

The tree squirrels chuckle, the flowers all cheer,
As he juggles his thoughts — what chaos is near!
His crown is made of spaghetti and cheese,
Bringing joy to the daisies that sway in the breeze.

A runaway pumpkin rolls down the lane,
Chasing the jest, igniting the rain.
With silly balloons, and confetti so bright,
He flits like a firefly, coloring the night.

At twilight's laughter, the moon starts to glow,
While shiny brass buttons align in a row.
In the enchanted embrace of silly delight,
We dance in this madness, a sparkling sight.

Threads of Serenity

In a world made of yarn, where laughter is spun,
The cat in the cradle, he plays just for fun.
With colors so vivid, in stitches we trust,
He weaves a warm blanket, from mustard to rust.

The polka-dotted skies, and the striped sunbeam,
Whisper tales of whimsy, like a nonsensical dream.
Each thread a delight, each knot a surprise,
In this tapestry of giggles, we find joy that flies.

With needles of joy, we craft silly art,
Giving life to our dreams, a whimsical start.
In the fabric of laughter, our spirits take flight,
We unravel our woes, in pure silly delight.

So dance in the laces, and twirl in the seams,
With threads of serenity, we stitch crazy dreams.
Wrap ourselves in humor, and laughter, behold—
The fabric of fun, in warmth, we enfold.

The Song Unwritten

In a garden of giggles, where melodies play,
A frog with a trumpet will brighten your day.
He croaks out a chorus of silliness grand,
As daisies join in, swaying hand in hand.

With a wiggle and jiggle, the butterflies sing,
They flutter and flitter, on whimsical wing.
A symphony of laughter, wildly offbeat,
As ladybugs tap dance to a comical feat.

The clouds play the drums with a pitter-patter,
While squirrels compose songs that just make you shatter.

Each note a tickle, each chord a charade,
In this song unwritten, we revel and wade.

So join in the revelry, sing loud, and be free,
With laughter our language, it's easy, you see!
In melodies silly, our hearts take a flight,
Creating the uproar of joy through the night.

A Dance in the Dark

Underneath the moonlight, we twirl and we twist,
With shadows of giggles, a dance that's hard to resist.
The stars are our audience, clapping in glee,
While owls hoot the rhythm, so wild and so free.

With shoes made of marshmallows, we bounce off the ground,
As laughter erupts, no sadness is found.
A tap here, a slide there, we tumble and roll,
In this comical chaos, we're losing control.

The trees sway along, with their branches in sway,
As we dance in a manner that's far from blasé.
With chuckles and snickers, we frolic so bright,
Stirring giggles and grins, in this magical night.

So join in the fun, come laugh and partake,
In the dance of the dark, let's amplify the wake.
With joy as our anchor, we'll spin 'round and mark,
The whims of the evening—our dance in the dark.

Tapestry of Inner Voices

In my mind, a chatty crew,
Gossiping over tea and brew.
One thinks they're oh so wise,
While another just eats fries.

The jester jumps, the scholar sighs,
One dreams of cheese, one of pies.
Laughter fills the merry space,
A wild debate on outer space.

Among the threads of joyful cheer,
A voice declares, "Don't come near!"
But then a puppet joins the play,
And suddenly it's a cabaret.

In this patchwork of delight,
Where each one fights to be polite,
A chorus of absurd refrain,
I laugh until I feel no pain.

Symphony of the Spirit's Embrace

Here we dance, a clownish crew,
Fiddlers jive in socks of blue.
The conductor's lost in thought,
While the flute plays a tune of rot.

A trumpet honks a silly cheer,
There's always room for a pint of beer.
The percussionists drop some beat,
And everyone tries to feel the heat.

A wobbly cello hums alone,
Dancing left while staring at the phone.
An octopus with juggling balls,
Wonders why nobody calls.

Each note a giggle, every beat a tease,
Filling hearts with giggly ease.
We're a riot, can't you see?
Just listen to our melody!

The Collective Song Within

A choir of quirks in my head,
Each one dreams of cake instead.
While some debate on how to snack,
Others plot a great attack.

One wants jazz, another funk,
While one just grumbles, feeling junk.
The harmony in this delightful strife,
Keeps me laughing through this life.

A pebble joins the merry mix,
A rockstar seeks to play with licks.
But dancing feet can't hold still,
An impromptu shimmy on the hill.

So let's all jam, let's have some fun,
Underneath that bright warm sun.
In this playful, silly throng,
Together we create a song!

Dance of Resonant Shadows

In the shadows, whispers roam,
Seeking laughter, finding home.
A ghost slips in, does a twirl,
With a wink, sends the room in a whirl.

The shadows bump, the echoes clash,
A playful race, a silly dash.
One claims they've lost a shoe,
While another seeks a scary view.

A silent film of oops and giggles,
As they dodge the light and wiggles.
They trip and fall, they snicker loud,
Their shenanigans—oh, they're so proud!

In this dance where giggles bloom,
We find delight in every room.
A shadow's laugh, a friendly call,
In this quirky ball, we all have a ball!

Trills of Forgotten Memories

In the attic of my heart, there's a tune,
With socks for instruments, we dance 'til noon.
Dusty old photos giggle at our quirk,
As we waltz with shadows, life's happy murk.

Laughter spills like lemonade poured too fast,
Each sip a reminder of the youth that passed.
We juggle our worries like clownish pies,
With whimsy and wonder, we'll reach for the skies.

Pillow fights echo, as giggles collide,
In a world where our silliness won't have to hide.
The clock chimes at midnight, we prance like deer,
Creating a symphony, with raucous cheer.

So here's to the moments that brighten our fate,
Where socks are our sneakers, we'll dance, never wait.
In trills of memories, forever we'll soar,
With laughter our anthem, let's always want more.

Aroma of Shared Journeys

Oh, the scent of popcorn on an old campfire,
Two friends with shoes stuck in mud, we conspire.
S'mores melting gently, a chocolatey dream,
We giggle, we stumble, riding the same beam.

Maps on the table, direction unclear,
We take the wrong turn, but we never fear.
With a playlist of nonsense, we bellow our song,
Navigating chaos, where we both belong.

Rain-soaked adventures, umbrellas fumble high,
Each drop adds a splash to our soon-to-be pie.
We chase after puddles like kids on a spree,
In this fun-filled journey, just you and me.

So let's pack our snacks, and hop on a bus,
With laughter our guide, come join us in fuss.
Aromatic adventures where every twist turns,
With silly emotions for which the heart yearns.

Poetic Interludes of Being

In the morning's light, we dance with our feet,
With slippers adorned, life feels oh-so-sweet.
Our breakfast of giggles, with toast on the side,
Every morsel savored, laughter our guide.

Naps turn to concerts, as dreams swirl around,
Silly serenades echo, lost in the sound.
With pillows as props, we perform on the stage,
Our worlds intertwine, like words on a page.

Out in the garden, we play hide-and-seek,
With flowers as partners, the blooms make us peek.
Each giggle a note, in a song so profound,
These moments, when shared, in joy will abound.

So here's to the jests, and the quirks that we find,
In poetic interludes, where hearts are entwined.
With laughter and love, we'll dance through it all,
In a world of our making, let joy be the call.

Elysian Echoes of Connection

Beneath the bright moon, we toss silly words,
Like confetti in air, oh, how it curds!
Our secrets like bubbles, they flutter and pop,
With echoes of laughter, that never will stop.

Time spins like a top, as we tumble about,
In a dance of delight, dispelling all doubt.
With snacks tucked in pockets, we venture anew,
Finding bliss in the chaos, just me and you.

Moments like fireflies, light up the night,
Each silly escapade, a spark of delight.
So here in this wonder, let's carve out our space,
With echoes of connection, and smiles on our face.

As shadows grow longer, let laughter be found,
In elysian echoes, our hearts will resound.
In this joyous adventure, we'll always be free,
With giggles and glee, just you, and me.

Revelations of the Heart's Chorus

A tune in my head, it wiggles and sways,
I dance like a chicken in peculiar ways.
With giggles and snorts, we jump to the beat,
Who knew my heart's song would lead to this feat?

A kazoo in my pocket, a trumpet in tow,
We march through the park, putting on quite the show.
Singing out loud, we cause quite a stir,
The squirrels join in, furiously concur!

With melodies stuck like glue to our brain,
We laugh at the memories that swirl in our mane.
A chorus of silliness, wild and absurd,
I swear, tomorrow I'll finally be heard!

So let's raise our voices, let laughter abound,
In this heart's little choir, we feel so profound.
With every note sung, we joyfully tap,
Life's a big jest, let's take off the cap!

The Unified Call of Existence

In a world full of wonders and quirky designs,
We spin in delight like the best of the vines.
A flip-flop in rhythm, we sway side to side,
As joy rides the waves, on this fun-filled tide!

With my socks on my hands, we declare it's a party,
A conga of llamas joins, oh so hearty!
They prance on the grass and ballet with flair,
Laughing as daisies whisper, 'Life's Merry Fair!'

We shout to the skies, "Dance like no one's near!"
The moon winks at us, "Let's shift into gear!"
In this glorious lounge of cosmic delight,
We twirl through the night, oh what a sight!

So gather your friends, and let's all be silly,
With hearts so light, and treasured, quite willy.
We'll sing our hearts out, in a beautiful throng,
Together we laughter, forever our song!

Harmonies Beneath Surface Skins

There's a tingle of chaos under each grin,
A ruckus of giggles where fun can begin.
With wigs on our heads and shoes mismatched tight,
We chapel down aisles, what a glorious sight!

Our shadows keep dancing like they've lost their way,
Imitating laughter that's begging to play.
With a wink and a nudge, we create quite a scene,
As we stumble through life, like a jolly brigade!

Beneath all the chatter, oh the tales to unfold,
Lies a harmony built of courage and bold.
From over-the-top hats to outrageous pranks,
We unify under the crazy, not thanks!

So grab all your pals, let's chase down the fun,
With harmonies humming till the day is all done.
In this raucous ensemble, we sing loud and clear,
Life's a riotous blast, and the end's never near!

Notes of Celestial Kinship

Amidst all the stars, our laughter does soar,
We clink our glasses and toast to the floor.
With cosmic confetti, we shoot past the moon,
This merry escapade is nothing but swoon!

With jellybean shoes and a tutu of fluff,
We dance with the cosmos; oh, isn't it tough?
Each twirl rounds a planet, we whirl through the air,
Sharing giggles with meteors, joy everywhere!

We chant to the comets, "Oh join us, please!"
They spiral and dive with a whimsical breeze.
In this orchestra of mirth, our hearts intertwine,
In a jingle that echoes, true magic divine!

So reach for the stars in your glow-in-the-dark,
In this silly circus, let's light up the park.
With notes of elation, we'll harmonize loud,
In this grand jolly fest, be merry and proud!

Cadence of the Inner Universe

In the circus of my mind, they play,
Juggling thoughts in a silly way.
The clowns wear hats of vibrant hues,
And dance to tunes that amuse the blues.

With every laugh, a spark takes flight,
Echoing adventures into the night.
The acrobats, they flip and spin,
As giggles bubble up from within.

A lion roars with laughter true,
As popcorn clouds drift by, too.
While tightrope walkers strut their stuff,
Admiring how the heart's never tough.

In this universe where joy's the king,
We find the joy in everything.
So let the music play and swell,
In this grand show, we all can dwell.

Embrace of Harmonious Whispers

Whispers float on the breeze of cheer,
Tickling ears that long to hear.
With giggles hiding in each line,
The world feels lighter, simply divine.

Like cats who break into a dance,
They prance and twirl, given a chance.
In secret corners, laughter hides,
Waiting for friends to come inside.

The whispers tease with giggles sweet,
A playful world beneath our feet.
Round and round, like a merry-go-round,
Inside our hearts, true joy is found.

So grab a friend and share the glee,
In this embrace, we all feel free.
Let chuckles rise like bubbles of air,
In this chaotic, dreamy affair.

Voices Entwined in Stillness

In quiet corners where voices blend,
Unexpected laughter finds a friend.
A stillness wrapped in playful jest,
Inviting thoughts to come and rest.

Between the gaps of silent sighs,
There hides a waltz where humor flies.
With whispers soft like clouds in spring,
Life gives us moments to embrace and sing.

Like tangled cords of mislaid dreams,
We twist in laughter, bursting seams.
A symphony of silly sounds,
Creating joy where peace abounds.

In stillness, find the playful muse,
Let every whisper be your excuse.
To dance among the rifts of time,
Where every chuckle feels sublime.

Echoes of Spiritual Amity

In the echoes of our friendly sparks,
We float like notes on excited arcs.
With cosmic giggles, we collide,
A universe where mirth won't hide.

From stardust tales and laughter's grace,
We chase the shadows, quicken pace.
A dance of joy, absurd and grand,
Together, we explore this land.

Like friendly ghosts in a playful spree,
We haunt the halls of harmony.
An echo of fun that won't deflate,
United in laughter, it's never late.

So let the echoes ring so bright,
In this spiritual, humorous light.
With every chuckle, our hearts intertwine,
In the fabric of friendship, divine.

Euphonic Threads of Life

In a dance of socks and shoes,
Life plays silly tunes, it's true.
With mismatched pairs, we prance and glide,
Each step a chuckle, in joy we stride.

The coffee spills, the cat's in flight,
Chasing shadows in morning light.
Choruses of laughter fill the air,
For every blunder, we still don't care.

A jolly jig on wobbly chairs,
The dog joins in, with floppy flares.
Wrapping us in a woozy cheer,
Even when the world feels queer.

With colorful threads, we weave and spin,
In goofy moments, we all fit in.
Embracing the quirkiness of our days,
In this chaotic dance, we find our ways.

Celestial Harmonies Unfurling

Stars shine bright in a quirky show,
Galaxies giggle, putting on a glow.
With asteroids dancing, twinkling bright,
A cosmic party, what a sight!

Aliens boogie with umbrellas wide,
Sipping space juice, they take a ride.
Planetary pranks and wobbly tunes,
Twirling around like silly loons.

Meteor showers rain silly beats,
While comets skip on youthful feats.
The Milky Way's a carnival bright,
In this grand universe, all feels right.

So gather 'round, with glee unfurled,
In this funny cosmos, we find our world.
With laughter echoing through the night,
Celestial dreams bring pure delight.

Whirls of Interwoven Journeys

With a compass that goes round and round,
We take the most absurd paths found.
Lost in a forest of tangled vines,
Chasing rabbits, crossing funny lines.

A bicycle ride on a noodle road,
Finding treasures in every code.
Dancing ducks and a singing tree,
Life becomes a hilarious spree.

The map's upside-down, what a twist!
But who needs plans? We can't resist!
Every corner brings a new surprise,
As laughter twinkles in our eyes.

So let's set sail on this vibrant quest,
With joy as our guide, we're truly blessed.
Every whirl brings tales to share,
In this merry mess, we find our flair.

Songs of the Inward Journey

In the mirror, a peculiar face,
Makes goofy faces, keeps up the pace.
Each quirk a tune, notes bright and bold,
A symphony of silliness unfolds.

Dancing thoughts like springy springs,
Whirling around in imaginary rings.
With giggles echoing in the brain,
Finding joy in the mundane pain.

Each self-reflection a humorous sight,
Comedic errors lend laughter light.
We trip on dreams, stutter on stars,
But every stumble leaves no scars.

So play along with this quirky score,
Embrace the flaws we can't ignore.
In the playful mirror, life's a jest,
In this inward song, we feel the best.

www.ingramcontent.com/pod-product-compliance
Lightning Source LLC
Chambersburg PA
CBHW050307120526
44590CB00016B/2525